Rookie
Read-About® Health

You Have
Head Lice!

By Susan DerKazarian

Consultant
Nanci R. Vargus, Ed.D.
Assistant Professor of Literacy
University of Indianapolis, Indianapolis, Indiana

Children's Press®
A Division of Scholastic Inc.
New York   Toronto   London   Auckland   Sydney
Mexico City   New Delhi   Hong Kong
Danbury, Connecticut

Designer: Herman Adler Design
Photo Researcher: Caroline Anderson
The photo on the cover shows a nurse examining a boy's scalp for head lice.

Library of Congress Cataloging-in-Publication Data

DerKazarian, Susan, 1969-
 You have head lice! / by Susan DerKazarian.— 1st ed.
    p. cm. — (Rookie read-about health)
 Includes index.
 ISBN 0-516-25879-6 (lib. bdg.)   0-516-27920-3 (pbk.)
 1. Pediculosis—Juvenile literature. I. Title. II. Series.
 RL764.P4D47 2005
 616.5'72—dc22
                                              2004015308

CHILDREN'S PRESS, and ROOKIE READ-ABOUT®,
and associated logos are trademarks and or registered trademarks
of Scholastic Library Publishing. SCHOLASTIC and associated logos
are trademarks and or registered trademarks of Scholastic Inc.

1 2 3 4 5 6 7 8 9 10 R 14 13 12 11 10 09 08 07 06 05

Has your head been itching all day?

You may have head lice.
Lots of children get head lice.
Head lice are tiny insects.

One lice is called a louse. A louse is light brown or gray.

Look at this louse close-up!

This girl is drying her hair.

If you have head lice, it does not mean you are dirty.

Even if you wash your hair a lot, you can still get them.

A louse is about the size of
a small seed.

10

Head lice suck blood from your scalp. Your scalp is the skin on your head.

This sucking is what makes you itch.

You cannot get head lice from a pet.

Head lice live on people's heads. You get head lice from other people who have it.

These boys could get head lice from sharing a pillow.

16

You can get head lice from sharing brushes or hats, too.

People with head lice have lice eggs in their hair.

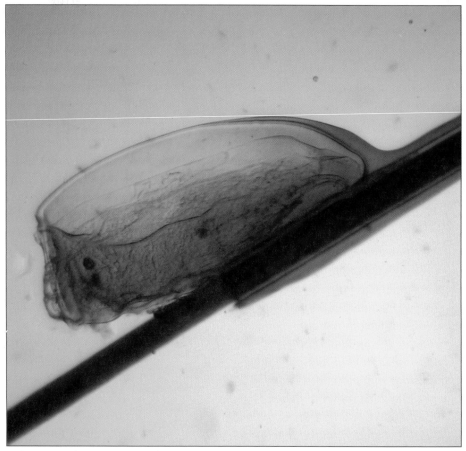

This is a lice egg. They are also called nits.

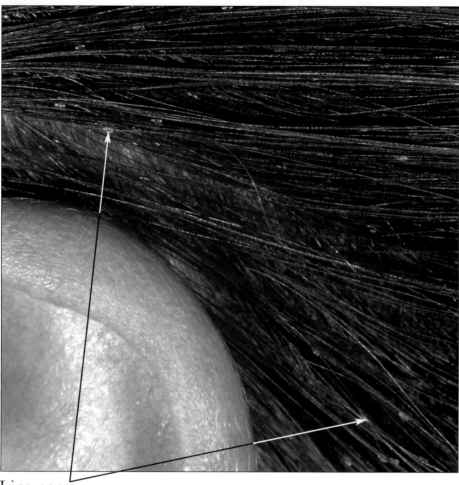

Lice eggs

The eggs are tiny and white.

How do you get rid of
head lice and lice eggs?

First, you must use special
shampoo to kill the lice.

21

22

Then, you must use a special comb to get rid of the lice eggs.

After the lice and the lice eggs are gone, wash all of your clothes.

Use hot water to wash the sheets and pillowcases on your bed, too. Hot water will help to kill the lice and lice eggs.

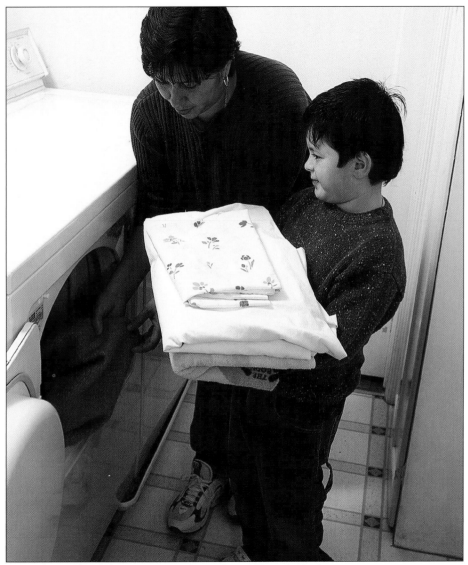

The heat in the dryer kills the lice, too.

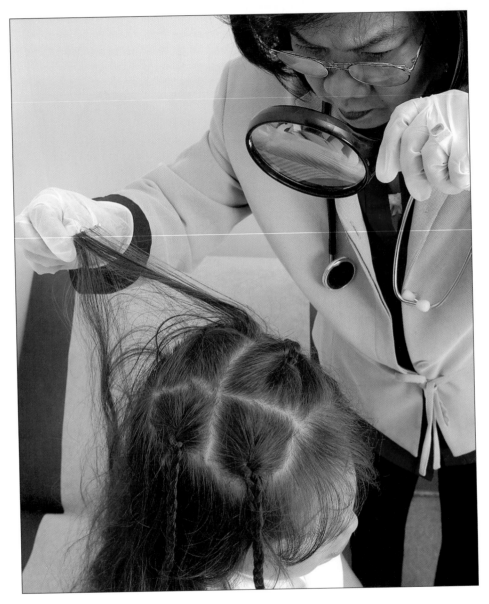

Many school nurses check students for head lice.

You should stay home from school if you have head lice. You do not want to give lice to other kids.

Don't worry. You will be playing with your friends soon!

29

Words You Know

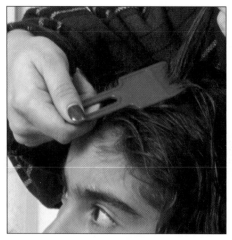

comb

hair

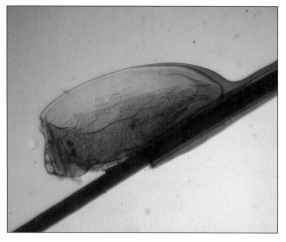

lice egg

louse

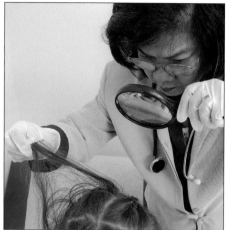

nurse

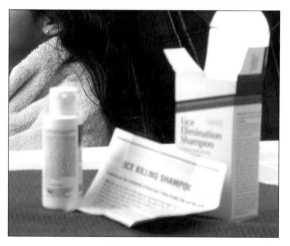

shampoo

Index

About the Author

Susan DerKazarian is a senior editor at a publishing company in New York City. She also writes many science books for kids. Her favorite things to do are reading, going to the beach, and hiking.

Photo Credits